AT THE WALL

RON AGAM

AT THE WALL

gefen
publishing house בית התצאה לאור

JERUSALEM ◆ NEW YORK

Photography: Ron Agam

Design: Guillermo Fridman

Edition 9 8 7 6 5 4 3 2 1

Gefen Publishing House Ltd.   Gefen Books
POB 36004   12 New St., Hewlett,
Jerusalem 91360 Israel   NY, 11557 U.S.A.
972-2-5380247   516-295-2805
E-mail: isragefen@netmedia.net.il

Printed in Israel

Send for our free catalogue

Library of Congress Cataloging-in-Publication Data
Agam, Ron, 1958-

At the wall / Ron Agam.
p. cm.
ISBN: 965-229-150-1
1. Western Wall (Jerusalem)–Pictorial works. 2. Me'ah She'arim (Jerusalem)–Pictorial works.
3. Jerusalem–Pictorial works. 4. Jews–Jerusalem–Portraits. I. Title.
DS109.32.W47A33   1997
9516.94'42 - dc21   97-31942
                                                         CIP

In memory of my mother, Clila

Preface
by Ron Agam

Photography is the art of capturing a moment. In the history of the Jewish people, a moment can be an eternity. This photographic book is intimately connected to my awareness of my people and their history.

The genesis of this work was when I discovered, as a young man, the work of Roman Vishniac: he had immortalized the life of the Jews in the shtetls of Eastern Europe before the Holocaust. I was emotionally overwhelmed. It was then that I realized my fascination and attraction to the same subjects.

Today, when I stroll in "Mea Shearim", I see the same faces, the same expressions. I can somehow transport myself back a hundred or two hundred years and imagine how my ancestors lived. This is my attempt at being a visual poet, a story teller, with the help of my little black box. In **At The Wall**, I try to capture the spirit of the people of Jerusalem, Israel's capital.

The story that I report through the eyes of my camera is the same story that Shalom Aleichem told in his short stories about our people. The daily rituals, the prayers, the market, the reflection of Jewish life. These pictures are a return to my ancestral roots. In them, I imagine a grandfather I never knew, a life I never experienced.

It is still too early for me to answer many of the questions that I keep asking myself about my people, but through my lens, I strive to seek the answer.

When I was a little child, I remember my Rabbi enlightening me with the importance of "Na'ashe V'nishma", which translates "We will do and then we will understand." And, maybe now, I accept the full meaning of these words with all my heart, mind and spirit.

Back in April of 1996, I met Ron Agam at the Jewish Heritage Week Celebration hosted by the City of New York. On display was a collection of his photographs in an exhibit called "The One Hundred Gates: A Celebration of Jerusalem 3000," which commemorated the 3000th anniversary of King David's establishment of Jerusalem as the Capital of Ancient Israel. I remember Ron's photographs and how closely they resembled the images still in my mind from my recent trip to Israel.

We are all familiar with the power of photographs. They can touch you and move you in ways words can not. Individually, his photographs are frozen moments in time, but collectively, they tell a compelling story about the struggles and triumphs of the Jewish people. From the leisurely young boys playing marbles on the sidewalk to the intense elderly man grasping his cane as he contemplates life, these photographs capture the essence of life in Jerusalem.

As home to the largest Jewish population in the world, New York City shares a special kinship with Jerusalem. Here in New York, we have some of the world's most significant Jewish institutions whose contributions are valued not only by our Jewish community, but by the entire city. All New Yorkers join me in celebrating and congratulating Ron for carrying on this tradition with his release of *At The Wall*.

Rudolph W. Giuliani
MAYOR

With A Wonderful Eye

On a thirteenth-century map of the world, with Jerusalem at its center, three continents surround the City of David. And on a sixteenth-century map, with the recently discovered New Land, America, located in a small corner, the earth is represented in the shape of a cloverleaf whose three petals, named Europe, Africa and Asia, unfold from a common Foundation Stone, at the heart of Jerusalem.

These visual figurations of the Earth follow ancient rabbinic legends which speak of Jerusalem as being the "navel of the world," much in the same way as the ancient Greeks revered the "Omphalos [navel] Stone" at Delphi. But whereas the latter has been restored as an archeological site, albeit loaded with mythological memories, three-thousand-year-old biblical Jerusalem has remained the living source of three monotheistic religions, the heart of a flourishing cloverleaf whose petals have never withered and, above all, the unsevered umbilical cord of the Jewish nation.

Whereas the daughter religions, Christianity and Islam, went out to conquer the world, the former building its sacred centers in Constantinople and Rome, the latter in Mecca and Medina, the exiled Jews carried with them throughout the Diaspora a "portable homeland," each synagogue facing Jerusalem as a miniature replica of the destroyed Temple, and crowning the prayers and hymns with an anthem composed some twenty-five-hundred years ago:

By the rivers of Babylon
There we sat down, yea we wept,
As we remembered Zion.

If I forget thee, o Jerusalem,
Let my right hand forget its cunning,
Let my tongue cleave to my palate
If I remember thee not;
If I set not Jerusalem
Above my chiefest joy.

[Psalm 137]

Having crossed many rivers and wept under many skies, remembering the glory and the ruins of their sacred shrine in the City of David, the descendants of those first exiled Jews gravitate toward the Western Wall as the natural site to send off their prayers and dreams to the King of Kings in Heavenly Jerusalem.

From all over the land and the world, praying pilgrims ascend to Jerusalem and its Western Wall. And there are those who live in its neighborhood, amidst their own spiritual and physical walls, dressed in the medieval garb of their Eastern European ancestors, oblivious to the Pathfinder on Mars and the Mir space station, as well as of the profane and mundane wanderers on land. It is among these that Ron Agam intrudes, not as an alien from outer space, but as the heir of a mystical grandfather who had his eyes set on the Lord's heavenly palace.

Wandering among men, women and children - who shy away from any visible camera in fear of being captured as a "graven image" by the magic lens - Ron Agam patiently and relentlessly focuses on a variety of them as they go to and come from the Wall, and at the Wailing Wall itself, frequently zooming in on some of them against a changing background. A daily world in black-and-white best captured in black-and-white, rather than on multicolor film.

Children caught in their schoolyard behind a grid of iron bars like happy birds in a cage, snapshots of a diversity of young faces staring at or trying to escape the photographer's inquisitive eye, furtive sketches of men and women walking on separate tracks and avoiding forbidden encounters, most of them unaware of being followed by their nemesis, the image-maker. All hurry to get to the Wall with the intent of hastening the coming of the Messiah in their own days.

A secret and symbolic thread runs between the man clinging to his hat - while securing a loose skullcap - and the lonely dove perched upon the Wall whose cracks are filled with fervent requests to the Almighty. A Jerusalem story is told that once upon a time a very poor man confessed to a rabbi the agony of his starving family; the saintly sage wrote a note, and bid the man to take it to the Wailing Wall, place it in an empty crack, then go home confident in Divine intervention. While he was on his way, a sudden strong wind blew off his hat, his skullcap and, alas, also the note. He returned to the saintly rabbi and recounted his misfortune, upon which the sage answered: "What more can I do for you, if Heaven itself does not stand by your side?" One day someone found the note on the street and, before returning it to the rabbi, read its content: *"Akhoti kalah, yonati temimah* ... My sister the

bride, my perfect dove [= *Shekhinah*, Divine Providence], I implore you, have pity on this man and provide for his family's livelihood."

A young boy, wearing a checkered shirt, stands between two men in long black overcoats praying at the Wall. A moment later, after one of the men has left, the boy is caught staring at the invisible camera, distracted from his prayers, his index finger pointing in the prayer book at the last word uttered, whereas his father has not moved an inch from the previous framed position.

At a different spot near the Wall, another man in dark garb, possibly a tourist - a camera hanging from his shoulder - seems absorbed in his prayer but holds a cellular phone glued to his right ear; does he have a direct line to the Almighty, or is he praying for prosperity while listening to his stockbroker at home? The silent camera records the irony of this acrobatic event; it cannot reveal the phone conversation.

With a wondering eye, in the complex tapestry of Jerusalem's people, Ron Agam has focused on a world of yesteryear frozen in time and space, which was once anchored at the eastern wall of a far away synagogue in a shtetl, but now nests in the vicinity of the Western Wall of the destroyed Temple.

And the man with a camera has replaced the Chassidic storyteller and the fiddler on the roof.

Professor Moshe Lazar
Professor of Drama and Comparative Literature
University of Southern California

1 The spirit

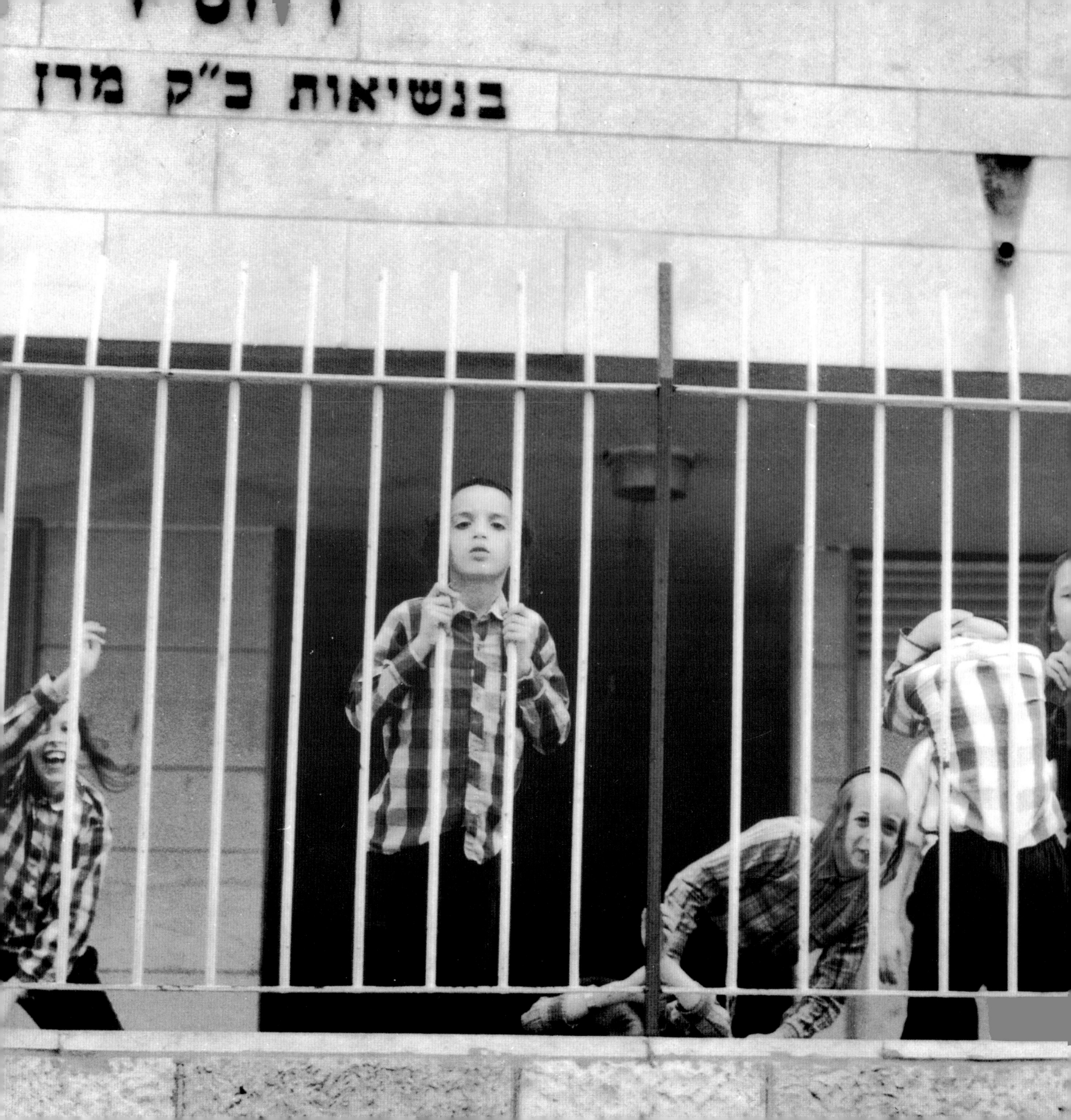
בנשיאות כ"ק מרן

◄ **2 - 3** Time out for a little fun!

4 - 5 *"Thou shalt not make for thyself any graven image"* Exodus 20:4 ►

6 A little charmer

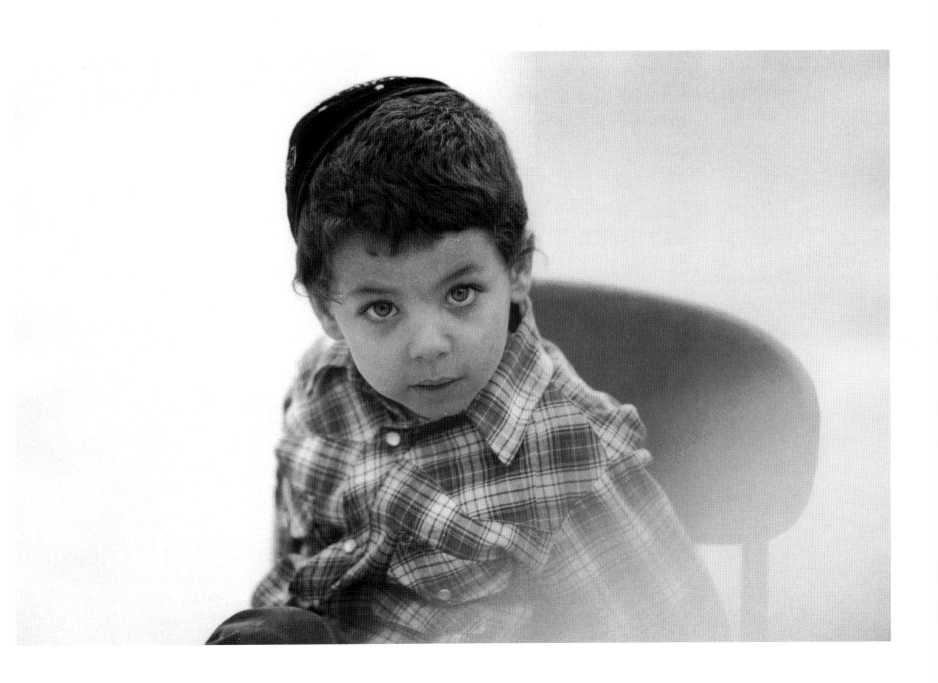

7 How dare you look at me?

10 Pious Yemenite boy

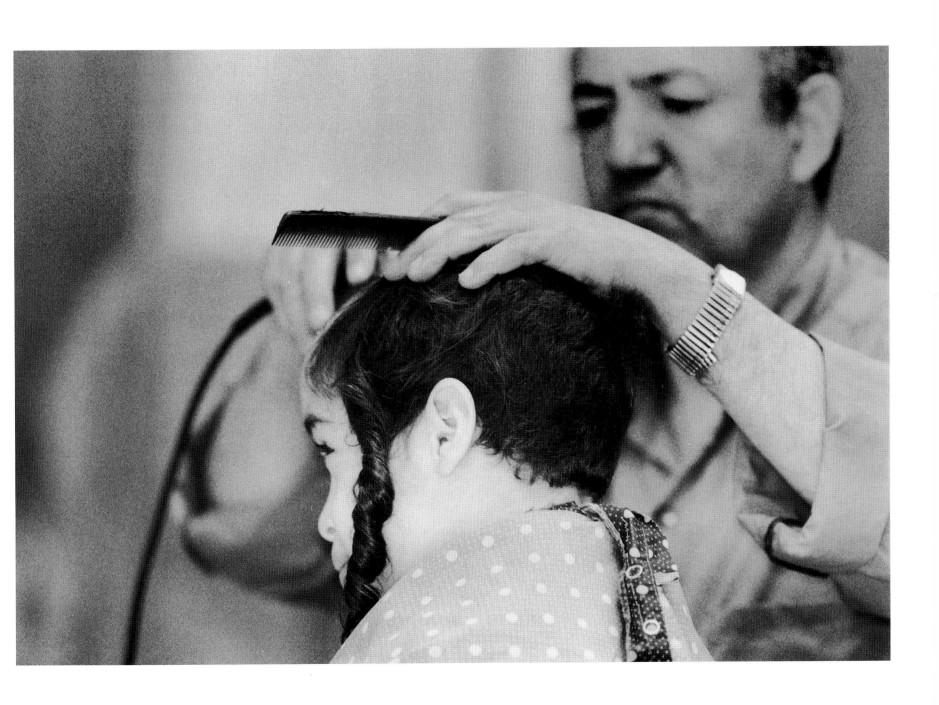

11 "Ponytails" - the Jewish way

12 A hug from a sister

18 Three generations

20 - 21 Ethiopian Israelis
on their way to the Wall

22 Will my prayers
be answered today?

23 Chassidic man
in traditional garb

24 Greek Orthodox priests crossing the Western Wall plaza

25 Prayer and water - the preservers of life

27 Reflective Yemenite

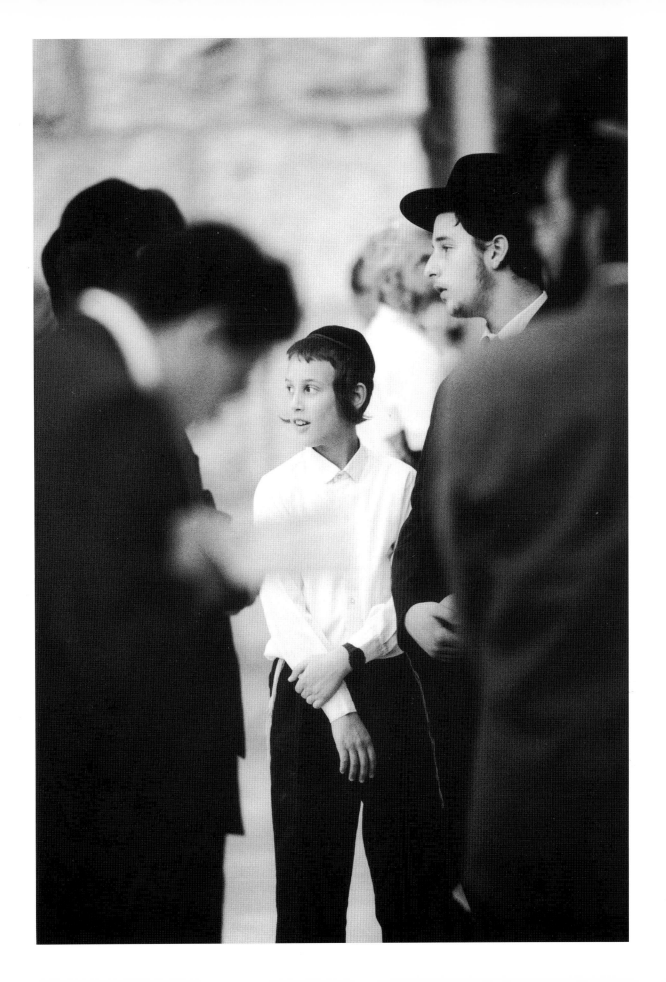

30 Women soldiers after praying

31 *"If there is no flour, there is no Torah"* Proverbs 4

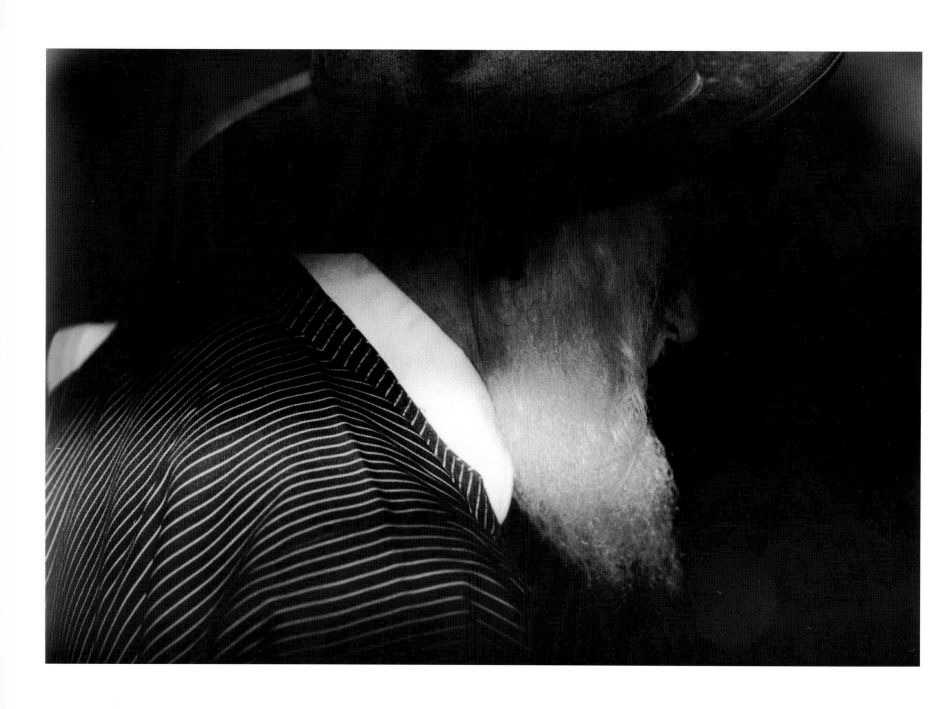

36 Will God send me more sorrows than I can bear?

40 A rear view

43 All secure

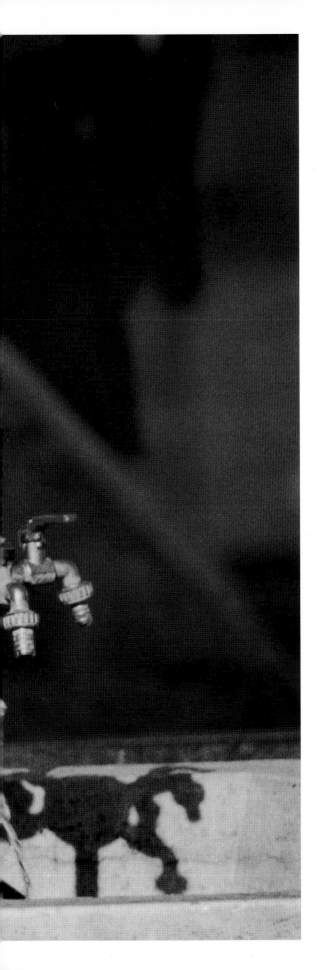

44 - 45 Purity before prayer

48 - 49 The kiss

51 A true believer

52 Women's section

54 - 55 *"Put off thy shoes from thy feet for the place*

on which thou dost
stand is holy ground."

Exodus 2:5

59 *"And thou shalt bind them for a sign upon thy arm..."*

Deuteronomy 6:8

60 - 61 Modern fashion
with ancient prayers

62 A direct line to heaven

64 - 65 Mass media in Mea Shearim (an ultra-Orthodox neighborhood)

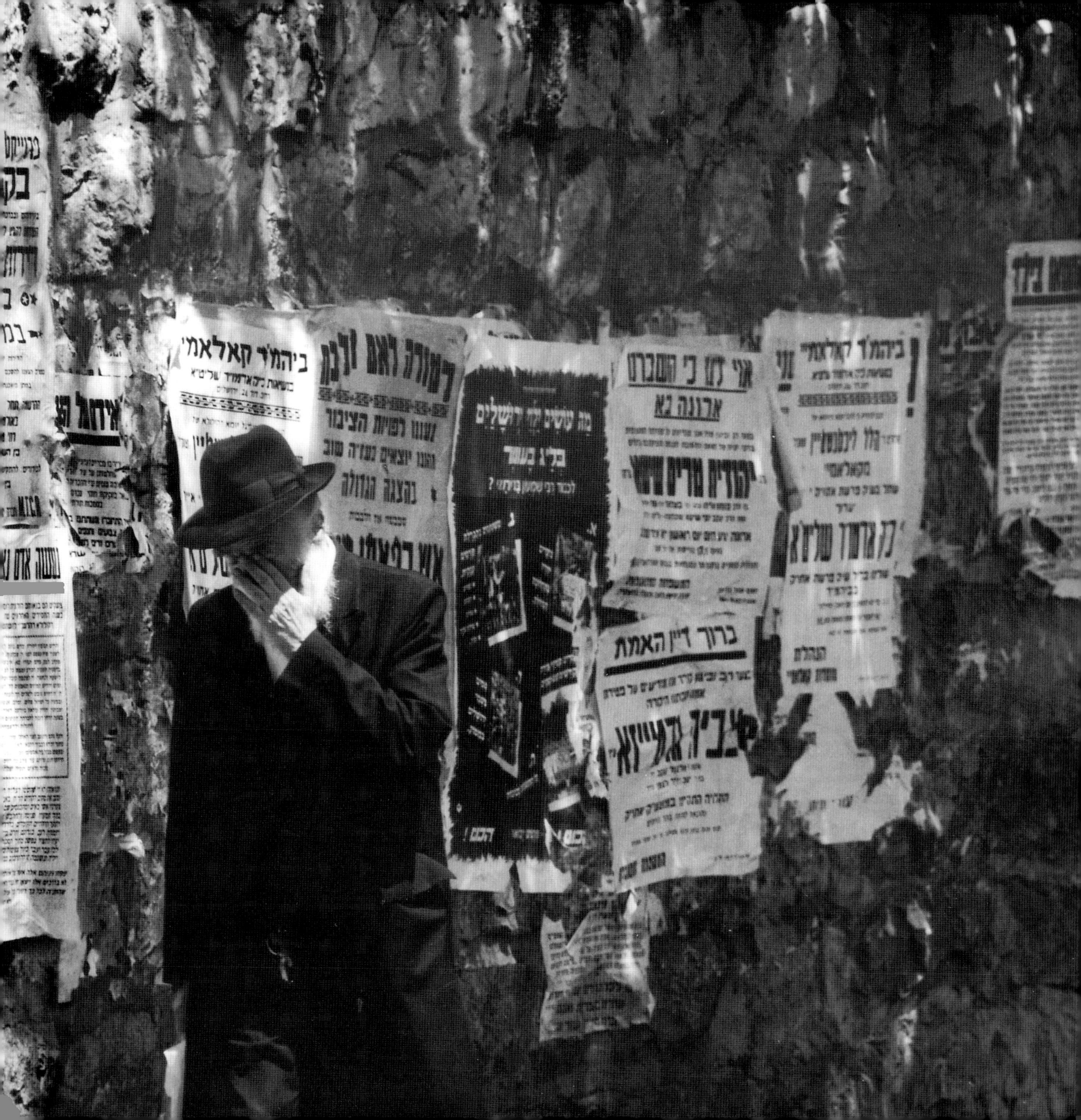
ביהמ"ד קאלאמי
ברוך דיין האמת
ביהמ"ד קאלאמי

67 Into the alley-away from view

69 Don't shoot!

RON AGAM

AT THE WALL

Back in April of 1996, I met Ron Agam at the Jewish Heritage Week Celebration hosted by the City of New York. On display was a collection of his photographs in an exhibit called "The One Hundred Gates: A Celebration of Jerusalem 3000," which commemorated the 3000th anniversary of King David's establishment of Jerusalem as the capital of ancient Israel. I remember Ron's photographs and how closely they resembled the images still in my mind from my recent trip to Israel.

We are all familiar with the power of photographs. They can touch you and move you in ways words cannot. Individually, his photographs are frozen moments in time, but collectively, they tell a compelling story about the struggles and triumphs of the Jewish people. From the leisurely young boys playing marbles on the sidewalk to the intense elderly man grasping his cane as he contemplates life, these photographs capture the essence of life in Jerusalem.

As home to the largest Jewish population in the world, New York City shares a special kinship with Jerusalem. Here in New York, we have some of the world's most significant Jewish institutions whose contributions are valued, not only by our Jewish community, but by the entire city. All New Yorkers join me in celebrating and congratulating Ron for carrying on this tradition with his release of *At the Wall*.

Rudolph W. Giuliani
Mayor of New York City

At The Wall is a collection of photographs of Jerusalem's holy Western Wall and its surrounding religious neighborhoods by Ron Agam, one of Israel's most celebrated photographers.

Through the eyes of his camera, Agam has captured the inhabitants of Jerusalem's ultra-Orthodox neighborhood of Mea Shearim and people at the Western Wall, one of Judaism's holiest places.

Album Size • Hardcover

Printed on 170 gr. chrome paper

73 black & white photos-duotone

$24.95

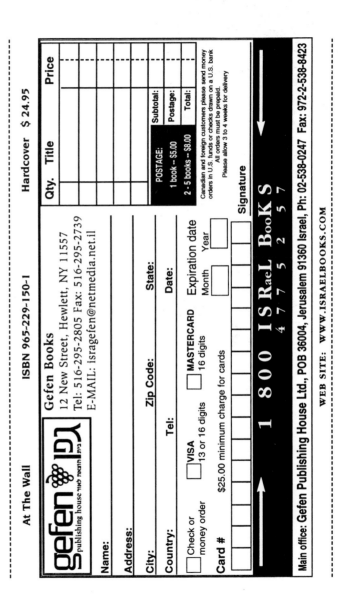

At The Wall   ISBN 965-229-150-1   Hardcover $ 24.95

gefen
publishing house בית הוצאת ספרים גפן

Gefen Books
12 New Street, Hewlett, NY 11557
Tel: 516-295-2805 Fax: 516-295-2739
E-MAIL: isragefen@netmedia.net.il

Name:
Address:
City: Zip Code: State:
Country: Tel: Date:

Check or money order
VISA 13 or 16 digits
MASTERCARD 16 digits
$25.00 minimum charge for cards
Card #

Expiration date
Month   Year

Qty.	Title	Price

Subtotal:
POSTAGE: Postage:
1 book – $5.00   Total:
2 - 5 books – $8.00

Canadian and foreign customers please send money orders in U.S. funds or checks drawn on a U.S. bank
All orders must be prepaid.
Please allow 3 to 4 weeks for delivery

Signature

1 8 0 0 I S RaeL BooKS
4 7 7 5 2 5 7

Main office: Gefen Publishing House Ltd., POB 36004, Jerusalem 91360 Israel, Ph: 02-538-0247 Fax: 972-2-538-8423

WEB SITE: WWW.ISRAELBOOKS.COM

"Ron Agam's photos are very moving.
I feel a deep emotional connection to them everytime I look at them."

Madonna

"With a wondering eye, in the complex tapestry of the Jerusalemite people, Ron Agam has focused on a world of yesteryear frozen in time and space, which was once anchored at the Eastern Wall of a far away synagogue in a schtetel, now nesting in the vicinity of the Western Wall of the destroyed Temple, and the man with a camera having replaced the Hasidic storyteller and the fiddler on the roof."

From the foreword by
Moshe Lazar
University of Southern California

AT THE WALL is a collection of photographs of Jerusalem's holy Western Wall and its surrounding religious neighborhoods by Ron Agam, one of Israel's most celebrated photographers. Through the eyes of his camera, Agam has captured the inhabitants of Jerusalem's ultra-Orthodox neighborhood of Mea She'arim and people at the Western Wall, one of Judaism's most holy places.

Ron Agam's work has been shown in numerous galleries throughout the United States. His photographs have been published in newspapers and magazines in Israel, Europe, South America and the United States. Ron Agam, son of Israeli artist Yaacov Agam, was born in Paris and spent his youth between France and Israel. Agam makes his home in New York City.

AT THE WALL
RON AGAM

Introduction by The Honorable Mayor Rudolph Giuliani

Black and White Photographs * Printed in duotone
Available from local bookstores and Gefen Books in New York

JERUSALEM gefen בן publishing house בית הוצאה לאור NEW YORK

POB 36004, Jerusalem 91360, Israel
Tel: 972-2-538-0247
Fax: 972-2-538-8423

12 New Sreet, Hewlett, NY 11557, USA
Tel: 1-800-477-5257
Fax: 516-295-2739

70 - 71 A sweet look

73 May her *kameia* (amulet)
bring her a little luck

76 A hint of affection

77 Shooting the breeze

80 - 81 Funeral procession for a Tzadik (righteous man)